A PERSONAL COLLECTION

America

by

Ray Madeline Van Dinther

For Kirran and Jessica

and Lydia and David and Owen

(and others to come)

ISBN-13: 978-1475285147

ISBN-10: 1475285140

2012

Other books in series

CHINA Down the Yangtze River

AUSTRALIA The Red Center

RAY MADELINE VAN DINTHER

"I like to make sketches whenever I travel.

I am constantly overcome with form, shapes and light and never feel that I can represent the beauty that I see. With and despite that knowledge, these sketches are my records and reminder to me.

I enjoy the process of making them and then giving them as gifts. "

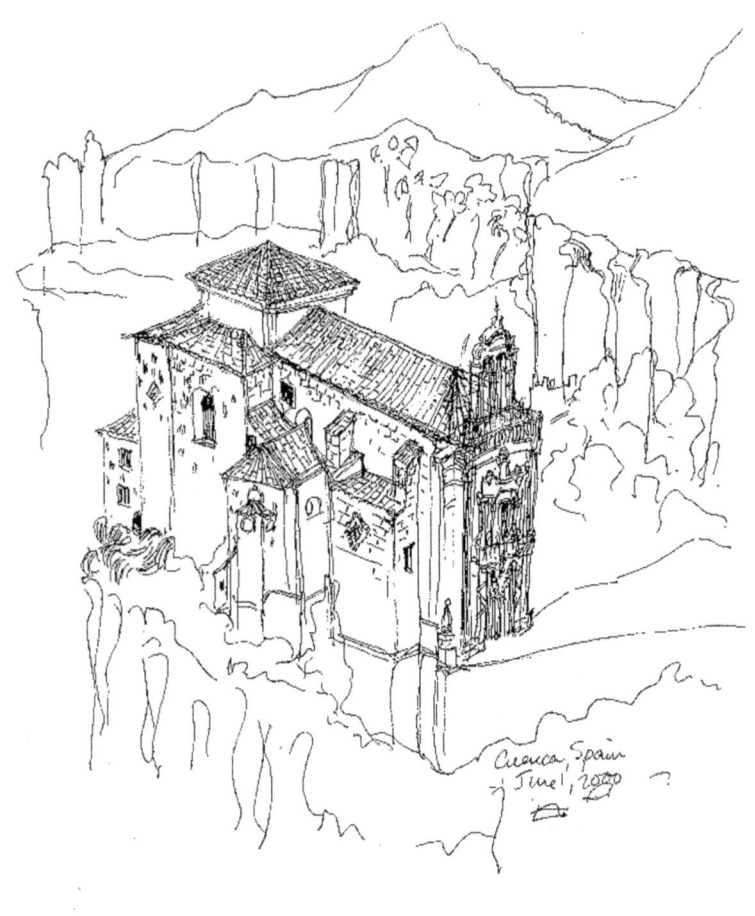

Cuenca, Spain
June, 2020

CUENCA, SPAIN
Convento de San Pablo

RAY MADELINE VAN DINTHER

"I like to make sketches whenever I travel.

I am constantly overcome with form, shapes and light and never feel that I can represent the beauty that I see. With and despite that knowledge, these sketches are my records and reminder to me.

I enjoy the process of making them and then giving them as gifts. "

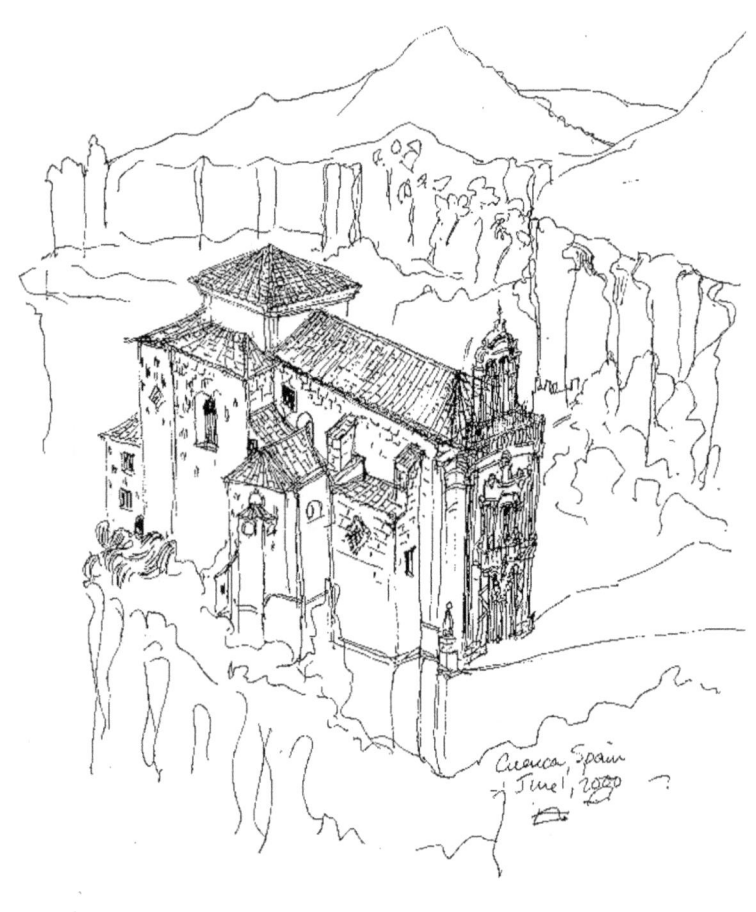

Cuenca, Spain
- June, 2020

CUENCA, SPAIN
Convento de San Pablo

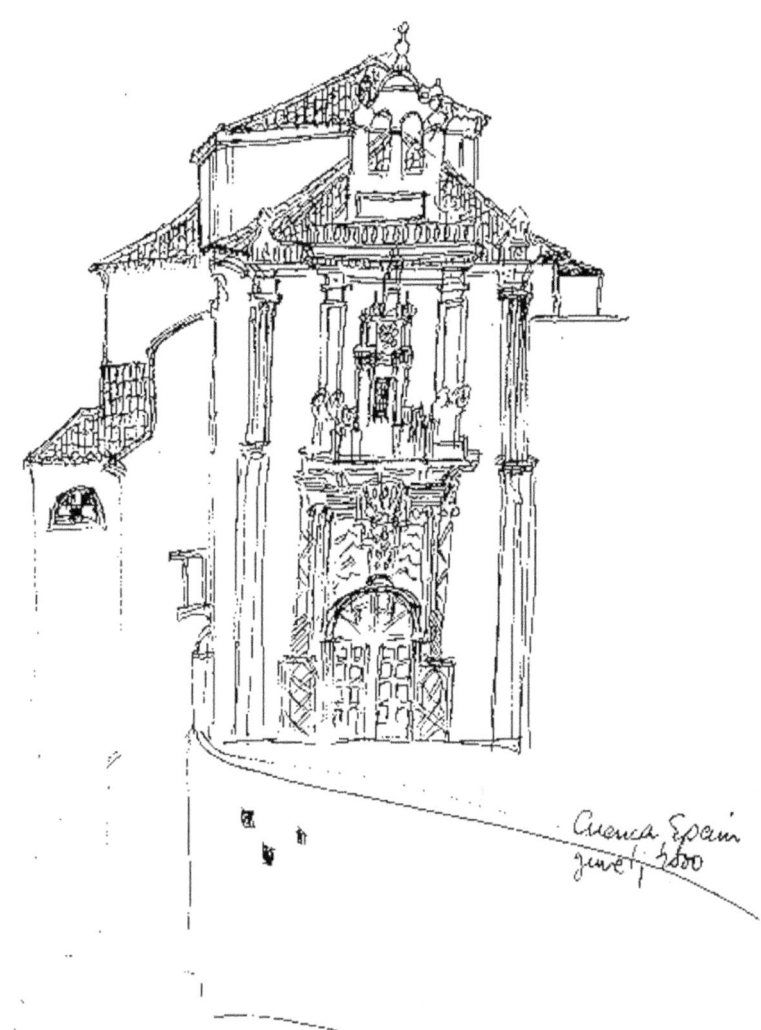

Cuenca Spain
June 1, 2000

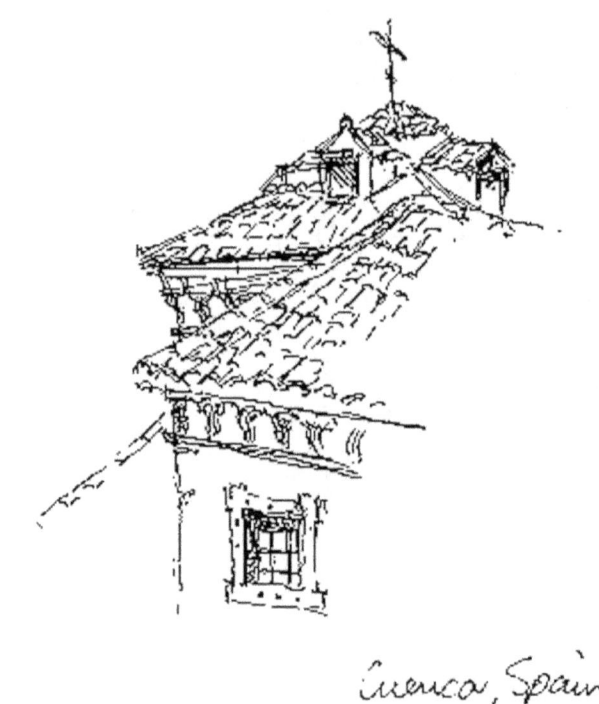

Cuenca, Spain
June 1, 2000

CUENCA, SPAIN

Hanging House

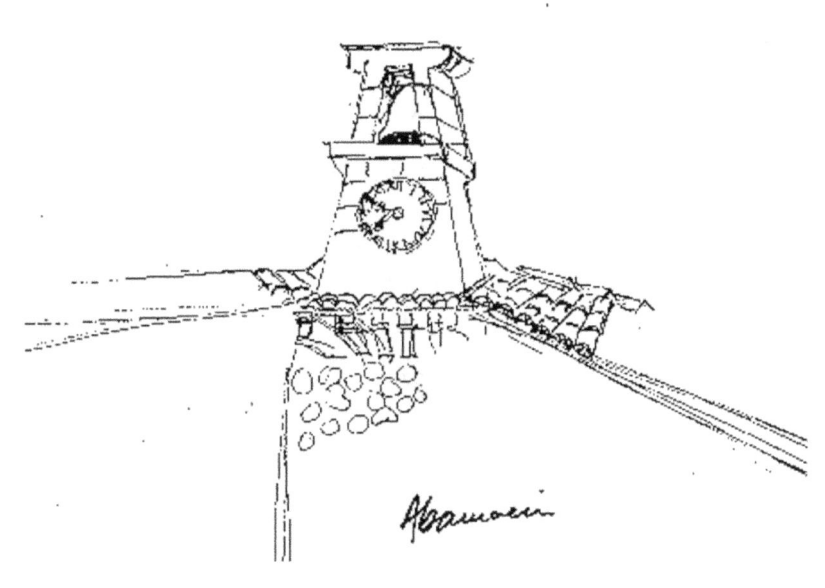

ALBARRACIN, SPAIN

Clock tower in the Plaza

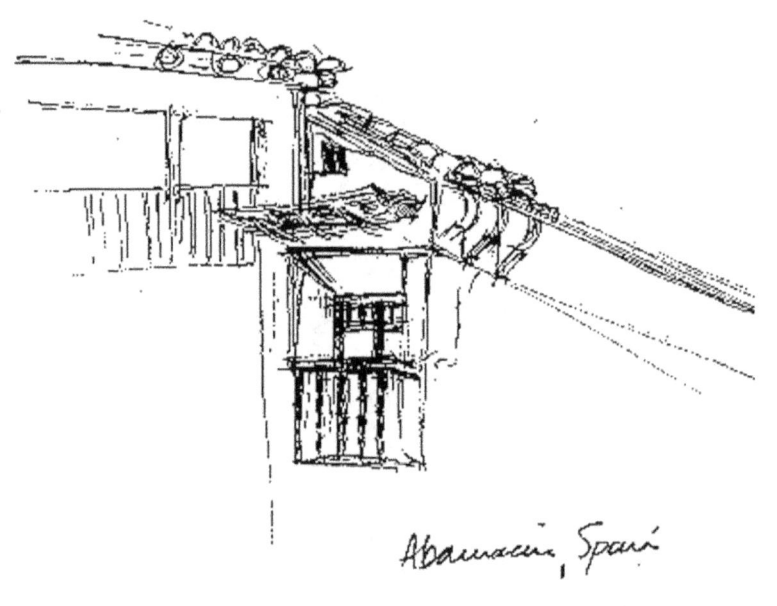

Albarracin, Spain

ALBARRACIN, SPAIN

Medieval housing

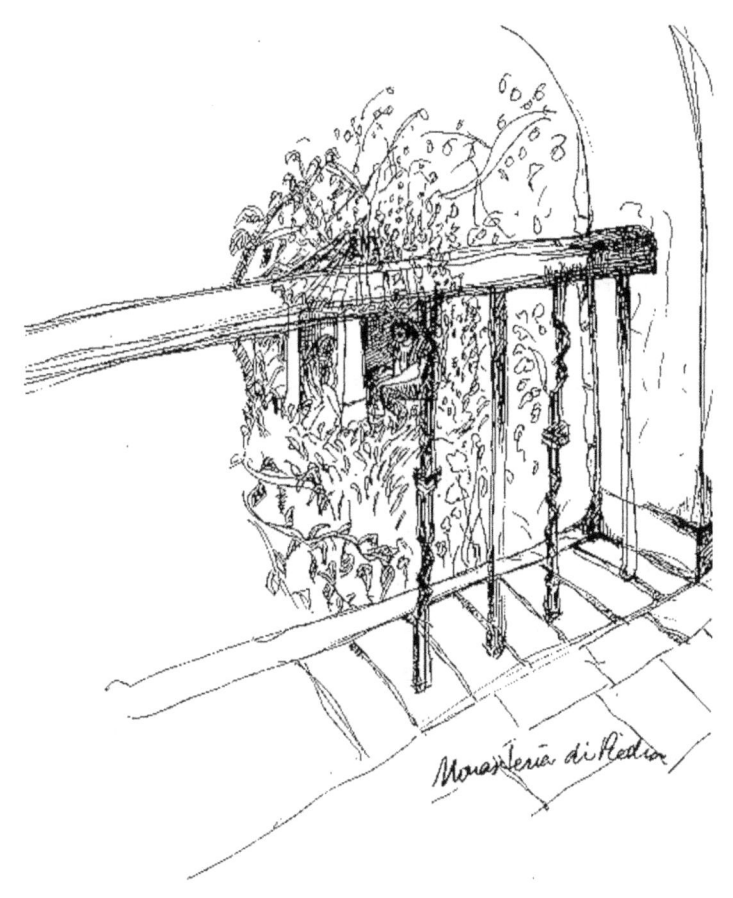

Monasteria di Piedra

NUEVALOS, SPAIN
Monasteria de Piedra

AMERICA

Behind our house there is a complex of ten tiny houses housing ten Mexican families. When I am describing how to get to our house, I say. "The large white Victorian house on the corner." Our house is really not that large but compared to the houses that surround it, it is rather grand. We bought the house six years ago, because I fell in love with it, when I first came to live in America. With a small budget I was looking for as much character as I could get and we found it. The house was a default bank loan sale and had been tenanted before we bought it. Before the tenants vacated they made holes in the walls and the ceilings and pulled the fence down; Had a party and left mountains of trash in the house. We stepped gingerly through beer bottles, leftover food and paper as we looked around the house.

Enamoured by the house I ignored its flaws and surprisingly after a thorough scrubbing and carpet cleaning and degreasing we moved in as it was and began years of fixing it up.

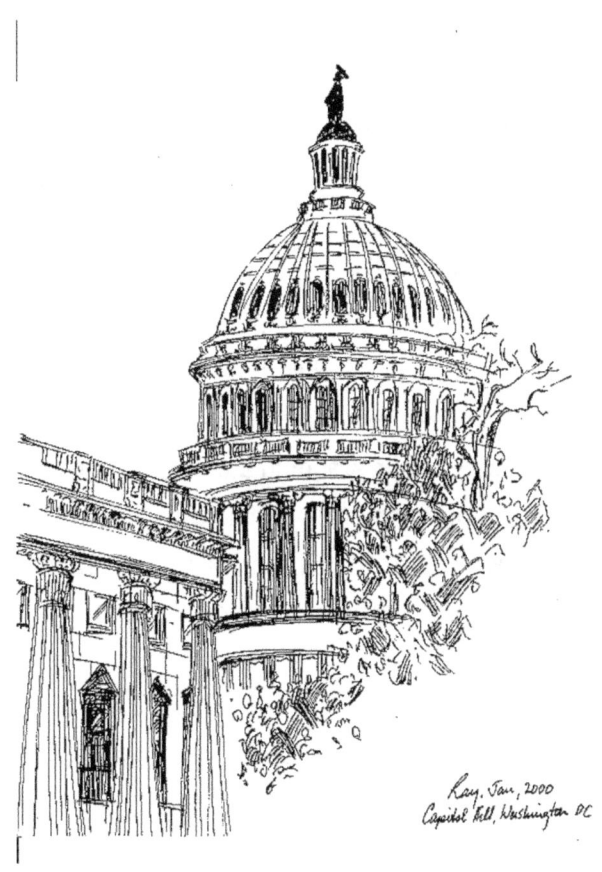

Ray, Jan, 2000
Capitol Hill, Washington DC

CAPITOL HILL
Washington DC

It is a never-ending process. As each task is completed we become aware of another two to be done. But the compensations are being able to see Los Angeles Harbor, the marina and past to the Pacific Ocean from every window in the house.

I woke up around two am last night thinking it was morning and realized a large spotlight was shining into the house. I went to the window and looked out to see a police car faced horizontally across the road towards our house with spotlights framed on two men standing against our front gate with legs apart and arms behind their heads. Two officers were in front of them, one on the radio to the station the other with his hand ready on his gun.

"Come over here nearer to my office and put your hands on the hood." The officer at the radio said. The two men walked to the police car and leant over the front of the car.

"Where's your ID". The officer demanded.

"Left it at home ". The men responded. One of them then spat on the road. -They're pretty cool about this-. I thought.

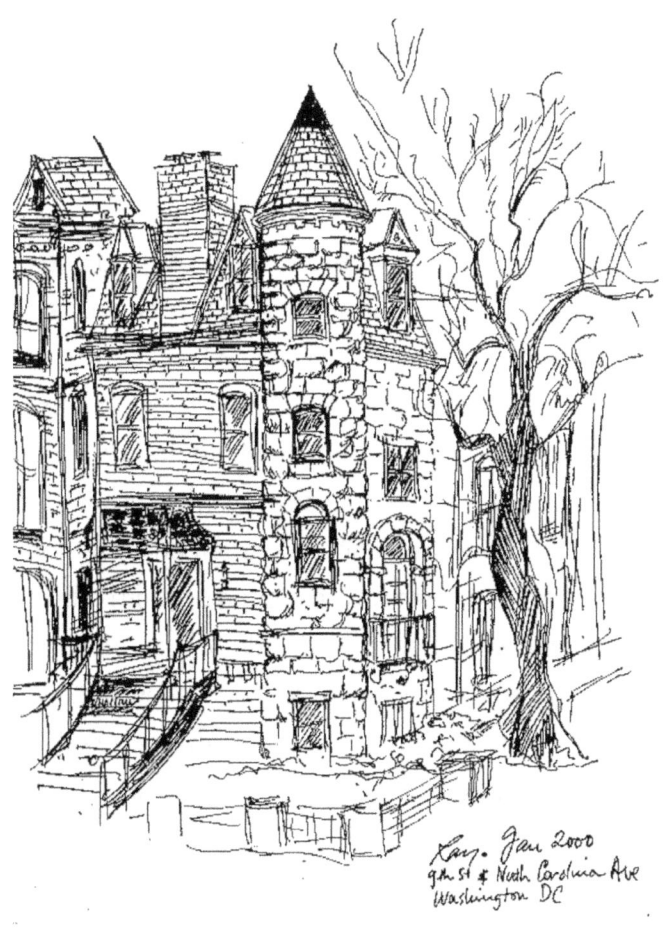

A HOUSE IN THE SUBURBS
9th St. & Nth. Carolina Ave, Washington DC

The officers spent some time on the radio then walked back to the front of the car. "Take your shirts off". He said. The two men took off their shirts and the officers examined the tatoos on the backs. of the two men

Twenty minutes or so passed and one of the officers suddenly turned to the men and said "Okay". "Go". "And don't let us find you walking around here again tonight". The two men put their shirts back on and sauntered off down the street and around the corner. I was surprised.

I was watering the garden one afternoon when a VW came racing around our corner being chased by a beaten up Cadillac. The Cadillac pushed the car up on the kerb just a few feet from where I stood hose in hand. A man jumped out of the Cadillac, gun in hand and pressed it to the window of the VW.

"Get out with your hands up and lie flat on the ground" he shouted. The fellow in the VW got out and lay flat on the ground in front of me. Meanwhile five police cars had also raced around the corner and there were guns facing me and my hose from every direction.

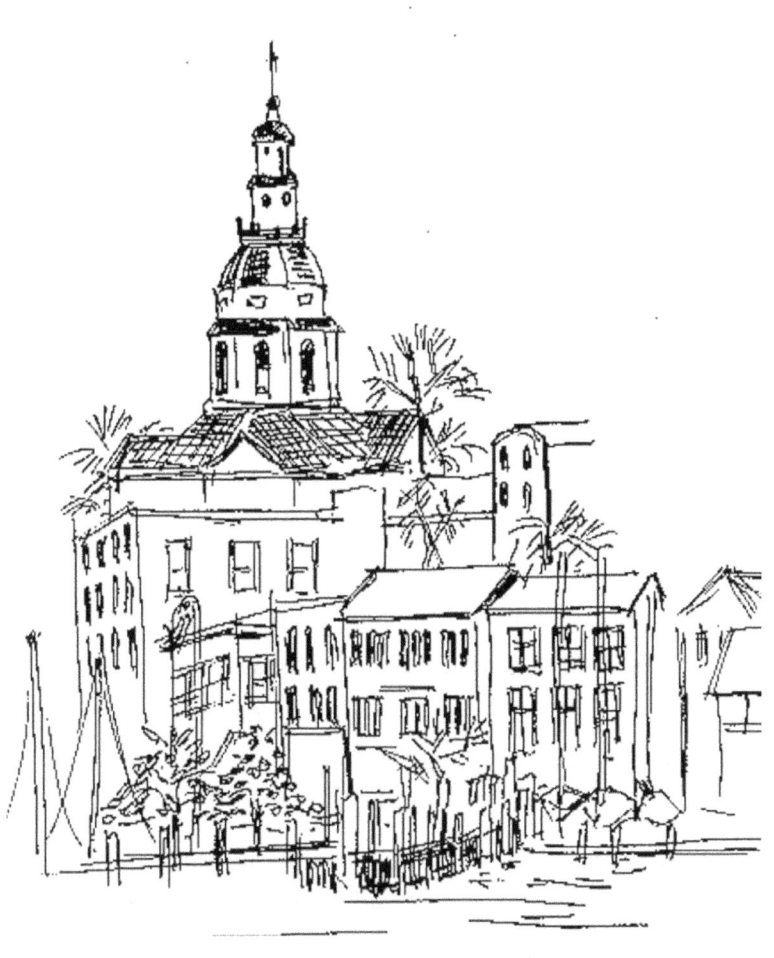

ANNAPOLIS

Maryland

In stunned silence I stood there, water flowing, until the fellow on the ground was handcuffed and the guns were put away.

The jean clad officer from the Cadillac then walked up to me, rested his hand on my fence, looked around at the ocean, turned back to me and said "It's a nice place to live, San Pedro." "Yes", I said, and finally I dropped my hose.

For a while there was a car business across the street. The owner had a wife on meth-odene. She would frequently sit on the street outside his shed at night shouting how much she loved him, hated him, never loved him. She would then start throwing rocks at all the windows of the building. One night she set fire to one of the cars and the police came and took her away for the night. But she was soon back with her shouting and rock throwing. They had some friends who came and parked their small trailer home in the street. One day a car pulled up outside our house and started shooting into the back of the camper. The camper left after that.

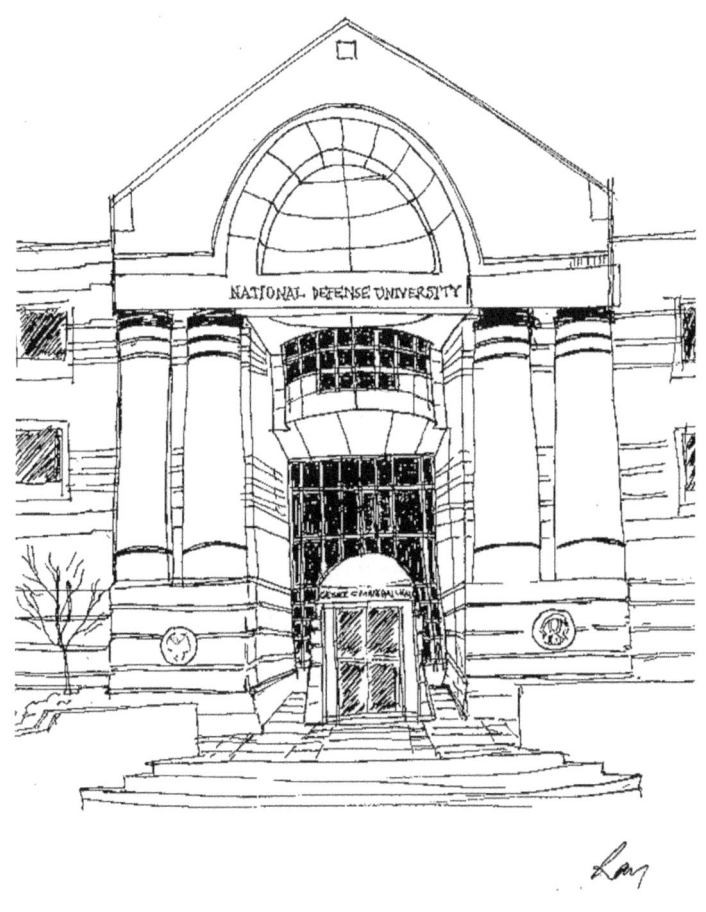

NATIONAL DEFENSE UNIVERSITY
Fort McNair, Washington DC

I have a little schnauzer dog named Hamish McDougal. Most of the time I call him Mr Hamish. I say he is my dog because after nearly six years John still refuses to acknowledge that Hamish is our dog.

Hamish turned up on the doorstep one morning when John was leaving for work. Not willing to leave a little dog wandering the streets I took him in and made signs saying 'DOG FOUND' that I placed around the neighborhood. I also put an advertisement in the paper.

"Be very careful what you write in your advertisement" the woman taking my ad over the phone said. "You know people come out and say it's their dog and then use them for experiments".

"Okay, I'll be careful", I told her. After about a week of John telling me I had to get rid of Mr. Hamish, I said "Okay, I'll take him to the dog pound". John was quiet for a while and then said "You know what they do to them after a week at the dog pound don't you?" I said nothing and did nothing. About two weeks later a car pulled up at the front gate and a woman leaned out of her car window.

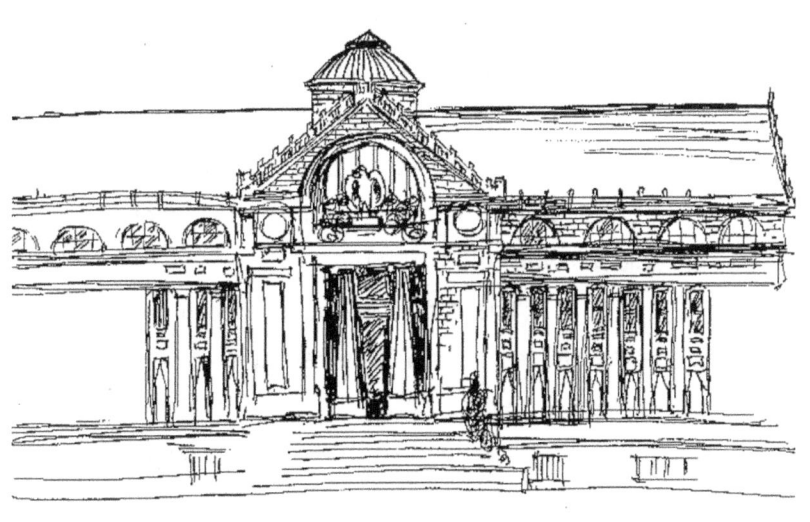

Kay. Jan 2000
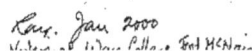

THE WAR COLLEGE
Fort McNair, Washington DC

"That's my Captain", she said. "But you can keep him, he suits this house". She then drove off.

When Hamish goes to the Dog beauty parlor he returns looking like a movie star, and is far too uppity for us. But within a couple of weeks he looks like a hood dog again, with whiskers stained and sticking out each and every way and his hair becoming matted. It reminds me of when dreadlocks were the fashion.

The effect of the chemotherapy made me nauseous for a few weeks and I couldn't stand Hamish's smell. I have felt better for the last two days and I don't mind his smell now. I am just tired.

Last night we took the boat out for a sail. I am not very brave about the sailing at the best of times but now as I am more tired and less able to react quickly I feel even worse about the whole process. When we left the marina it was very calm and peaceful but as soon as we got into the main harbor the wind started gusting and we hoisted the sails and cut the motor. Neither of us is very experienced, we are new sailors.

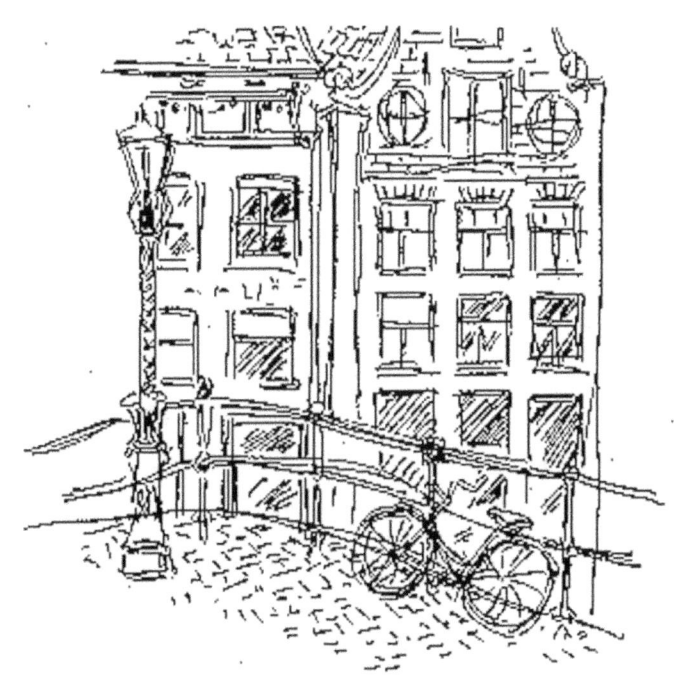

22 nd Feb. '97
Amsterdam

AMSTERDAM-HOLLAND

The first time we went out we didn't have a clue what we were doing and with our legs covered to our knees with sea water we nearly capsized the boat in the main Los Angeles channel.

Anyway we sailed around in the channel for a while in the ever increasing gusts and then I said to John "There's a whale". "No", he said, "It's only a seal". He knew I was feeling nervous and put my sighting down to fear.

"No", I said, "There's a whale". I was watching it spout and saw the tail fluking. He followed my line of sight and was astounded to see that I was in fact correct.

We sailed over closer to it and were totally in awe. It was a giant whale, at least thirty to forty feet long. I kept thinking of Loch Ness monster stories and wondered whether he would emerge underneath us throwing our boat into the never never.

He slowly rose up through the water and dived down. His huge body gliding through the water. He was truly enormous. We watched him for a while and then the mist started coming down from the hills and across the water. It became very cold and we headed back to the marina.

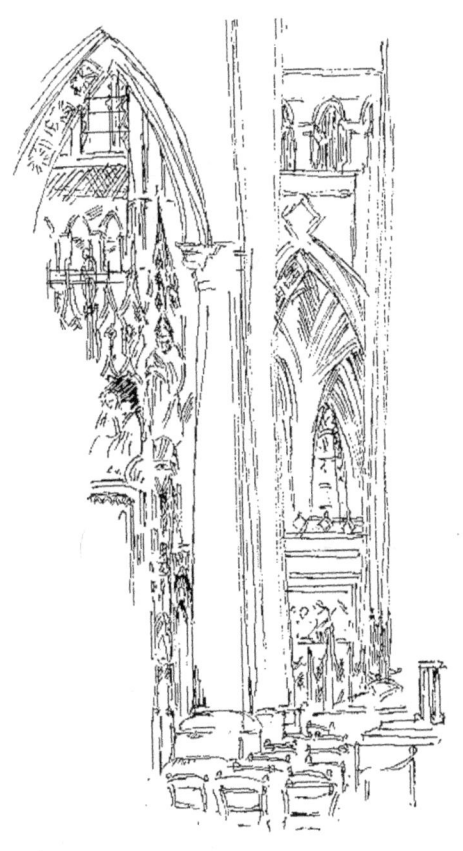

Chartres
24/2/97

CHARTRES CATHEDERAL
France

By the time we motored in the sun was setting and the light was filtering through the water and the myriad of other boats with shades of pink and yellow. It was still and quiet. I was sulking a little as we took the sails in and did the necessary tasks to finish up. Upset that I was not braver. Cross that I couldn't just attack the whole process with gusto.

Today, my head is telling my body that I am still bobbing up and down. This feeling of unbalance seems much more pronounced than usual.

A movie is being made down the road. I will go down there for a while and watch them. This is a pilot for a television soap. As I watched them play acting out a shooting scene over and over, I couldn't help feeling how bizarre to spend all this money and utilize all these people for a thirty second shot, especially when all around the real thing – shooting that is - is occurring.

The movie people frequently make movies in San Pedro. A couple of years ago they rented our house for their film making. They set up cameras all around the house and gave us lots of money to stay away.

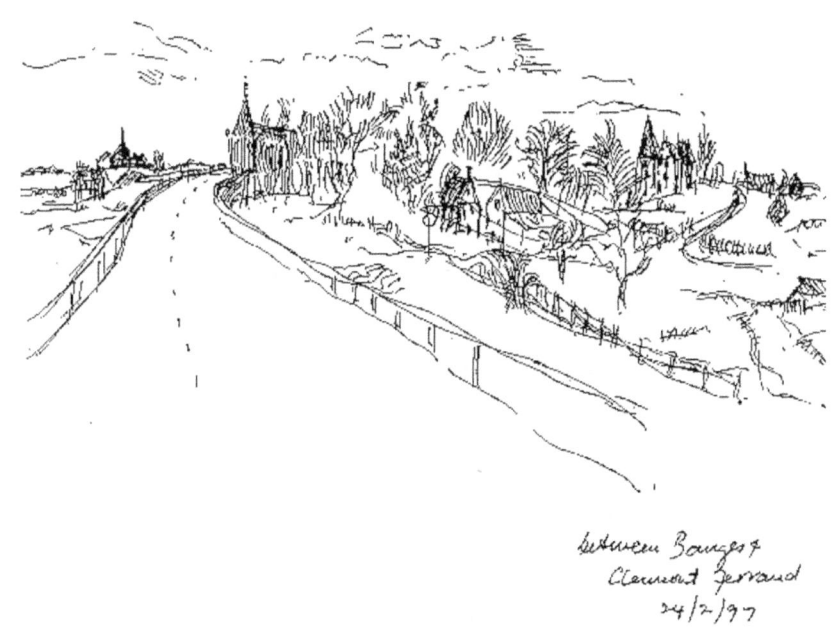

Between Bourges &
Clermont Ferrand
24/2/97

DRIVNG IN FRANCE

Between Bourges and Clement Ferraud

I feel better today but have had a rough week with the Chemo. When I go in for treatment I usually feel so sick that I start crying. They now think I'm neurotic and want me to take a tranquilizer before I go in. I hate the place, just the thought of it makes me feel bad. But really they are very sweet and I know they are making me better. It's just so ugly the whole thing. And me, I am not good at being sick. Sometimes John comes with me, sometimes Kirran. I don't think I can do it alone. But then I do. I always choose a chair near the door. It makes me feel I can bolt if I want. It's like I have a football game going on inside me. One side is playing to keep the other side out. One side says this stuff is out to poison me and the other side is saying - wait a minute this stuff is fighting off the wicked cells. And so the battle goes.

A week ago a noise woke me in the night. It was a thumping noise. I got up and looked outside the window thinking that I would see somebody in the street but I couldn't see anything or anybody. Then my attention was drawn to the deck outside the bedroom window and sitting in the corner of the deck eyeing me was a large round raccoon.

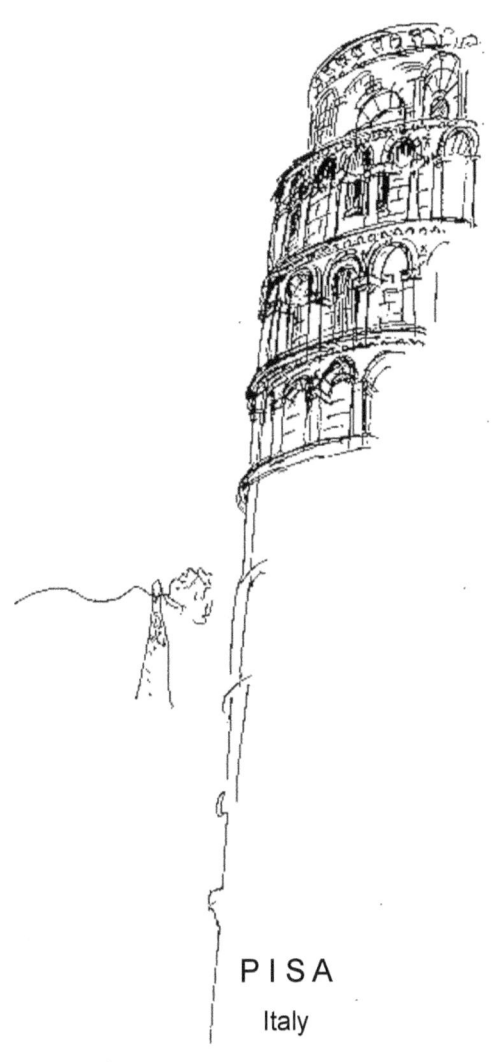

P I S A

Italy

He suddenly jumped up to the railing around the deck and ran away across the roof. I haven't seen him since.

Two days ago when John was feeding the fish in our newly installed fish pond in the garden, a pile of dirt had been dug up around the pond. John instantly accused Hamish of the damage and threatened to turn the hose on him if he came anywhere near the area again. When we installed the pond we bought ten gold fish from the local pet store at twenty-two cents apiece, brought them home in a plastic bag and spent a long time working out how best to acclimatize the fish to the water. Finally we added some hot water to warm the pond. One fish died a few days later, was buried and nine have since thrived, getting visibly larger daily.

Because I have to drink vast quantities of liquid since beginning chemotherapy I have to get up to use the bathroom three or four times a night. (How American I have become, I no longer say toilet.) Last night when I got up just before midnight I listened to the water splashing back into the pond that John had made. The water ran down the waterfall through the ferns in the garden.

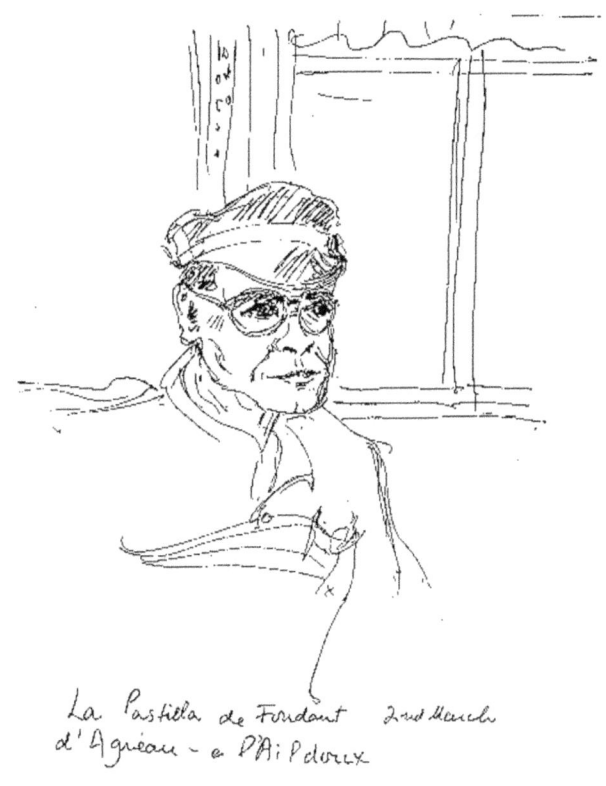

La Pastilla de Fondant d'Agneau — a D'Aipdoux 2nd March

'POP'e D'AIPDOUX

La Pastilla de Fondant d' Agneau

I got up again at four am and this time I couldn't hear the trickle of the water over the rocks. I opened the window and looked down into the garden through sleepy eyes but couldn't see clearly so I went downstairs and picked up the torch (flashlight in American) and tried to see whether the water had gone down in the pond. Finally I went outside. There was no water moving through the pump. The pond water was half depleted and murky green and dirty. Rocks and bark had been pushed into the pond and there was dirt piled everywhere and I couldn't see any fish. The pump was not working, no water was coming down the waterfall. In fact the pond and surrounds had been decimated and Hamish was asleep inside the house.

'The raccoon.' I suddenly realized, He has also eaten my fish. So far, I cannot tell how many, as the water that is left in the pond is too churned up and dirty to see through

He has eaten seven of our goldfish out of the pond.

Today I went to the SPCA and rented a trap.

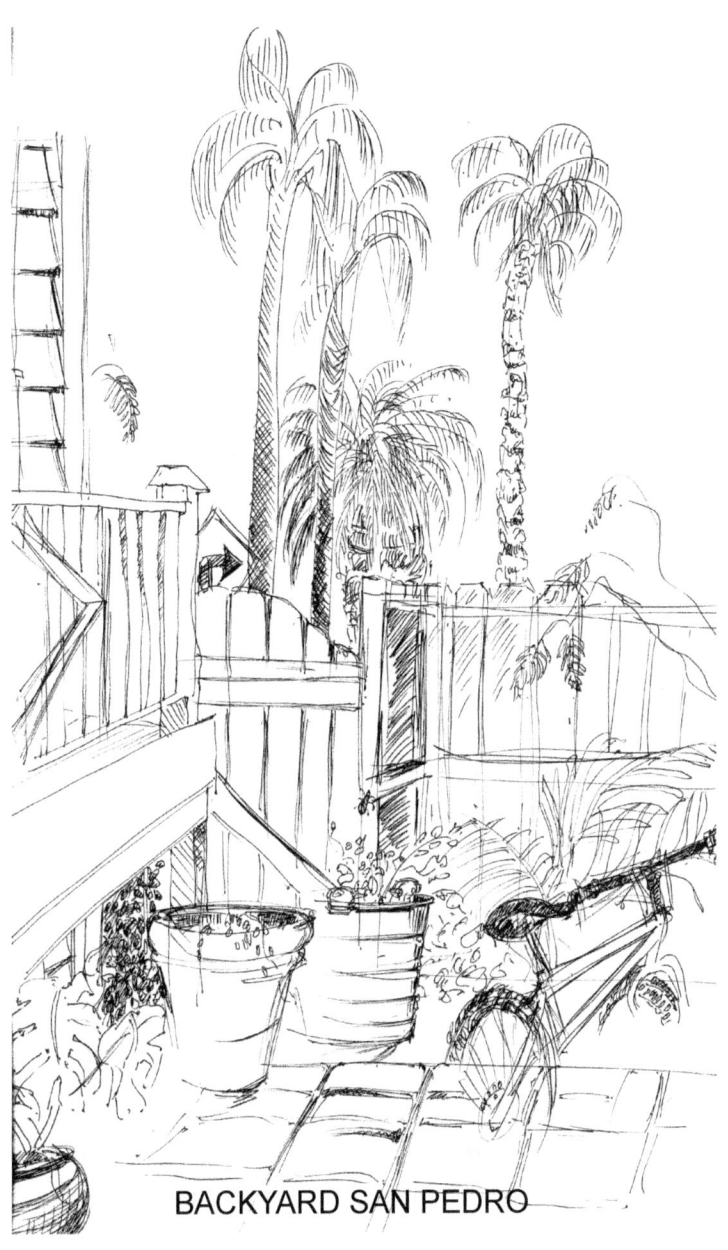

BACKYARD SAN PEDRO

But I feel a bit mean. What if it's a she and she has babies to feed?

We set the cage for him (her?) last night, to catch and relocate him. But he must have thought 'Hmmmmm.......... Supper'. He stretched his paw in and took 2 peanut butter sandwiches without tripping the door and then dug up the garden again.

We reset the cage again last night and this morning, there was the racoon fighting to get out of the trap.

What a beautiful creature, and clever too, as he tried to undo the flaps of the cage. But the double doors 'out-raccooned' him. We placed the cage holding the raccoon in the back of the car and drove him to Palos Verdes, where there is lots of scrub. I kept looking back at him. He was sitting quietly in the cage looking at me intently. His cute little bear ears pricked up wondering what fate was in store for him.

We released him from the cage into a scrubby area with a little stream nearby.

'You've moved up the hill little raccoon." I told him. "That's more than we can afford to do."

Saturday 9th November

Sitting on the back step of the Ford
somewhere east of Palm Springs.
Surrounded by mountains & fast food.
Hi hot - I have found a tree to park
under while I sit under a McDonalds sign
Part of me feels liberated - part of me sad
that I am here alone & John has gone
to Africa alone.

DRIVING TO ARIZONA

Yesterday, I got a shock. I had been feeling tired as I walked through Home Depot with John. Suddenly I had to sit down. I found an empty forklift at the back of the store and sat down on the edge waiting for John to buy some concrete. I felt like crying. That made me remember that I had forgotten to go to the treatment (euphemism for cancer) center for my weekly blood test. When John found me I told him that we should go to the center even though I was late.

When I had my blood test they told me my white cell count was very low and I would have to be very careful of any possible bacterial infections. My teeth had been aching a lot so they have put me on antibiotics.

Mentally this has pushed me to another place now. I have been cruising along thinking this is not really a problem. Sick for a couple of weeks and then not sick. But now, I am feeling scared. I am in my own little vacuum looking at everybody and everything as a potential threat. I also have this feeling that I am alien from everybody around me as they are all healthy.

I don't want to be sick.

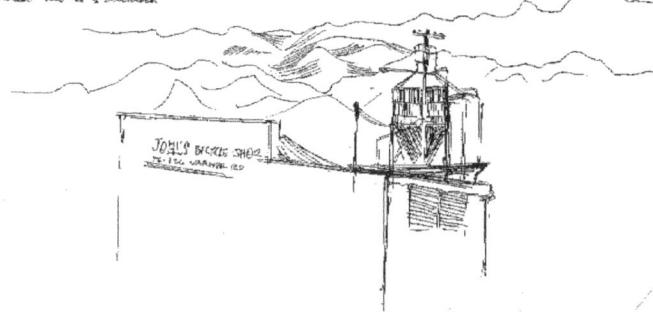

Love is such a tenuous thing. there are
no guarantees that it will continue - apart
from the love between mother & children.

On the other side of these mountains
is Los Angeles. There are so many millions
of people there who have never been to this side of the mountains

DRIVNG TO ARIZONA

Saturday evening
What horror - the car lost power
& stopped on the freeway where the 10
split off to Los Angeles. I was right
on the bend with about 4' of side
and 4' of car sticking out on the road.
With hazard lights flashing I crawled out
in an 8" space fearing that cars would
crash into me. I tried to wave cars down
for half an hour. 2 stopped but could do
nothing - The 3rd saw a tow truck coming &
waved him over - I had visions of being
towed back to LA. The tow truck driver
started the car - said it idled well - went to
the throttle and found the throttle cable off -
wonderful man - he fixed it - I gave him $10-00
and started again in the dark.
I am lying in the back of the car near at
Don Denellays - WOW. This is a horse factory -
I am parked outside a shade - nearby is one of
the workers. This is strange & isolated - dust,

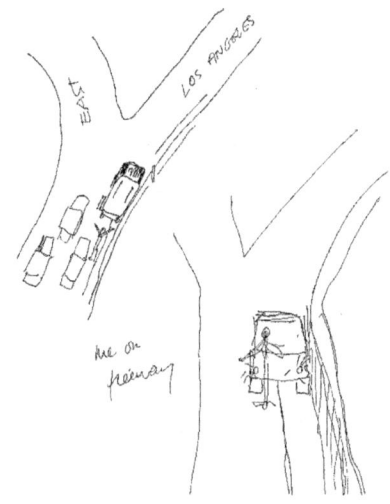

PHOENIX ARIZONA

So far, as much as possible I have kept this whole illness at a distance. Apart from the depressing reality check at the cancer center. Now it will be more difficult to do that. I have thoughts about my mortality that I don't really want to have. I have to shake myself out of it.

There are now two raccoons. I don't know if one of them is the original back with a partner. But they are creating havoc. We put another batch of fish in the pond. Around forty in all. We have six left. I also put a water lily in but that was dug up as well. John put a beautiful turquoise beta fish in and they ate it on his first night. Every evening now I cover the pond but they keep digging up the garden and reaching in to grab the fish. John tells me to get more cages but I have given up. I think it is easier to change our expectations than to try and mould the environment to our needs. I'm sure there is a never ending supply of raccoons discovering our pond in dry San Pedro.

This morning I looked out at the fish pond and saw chaos.

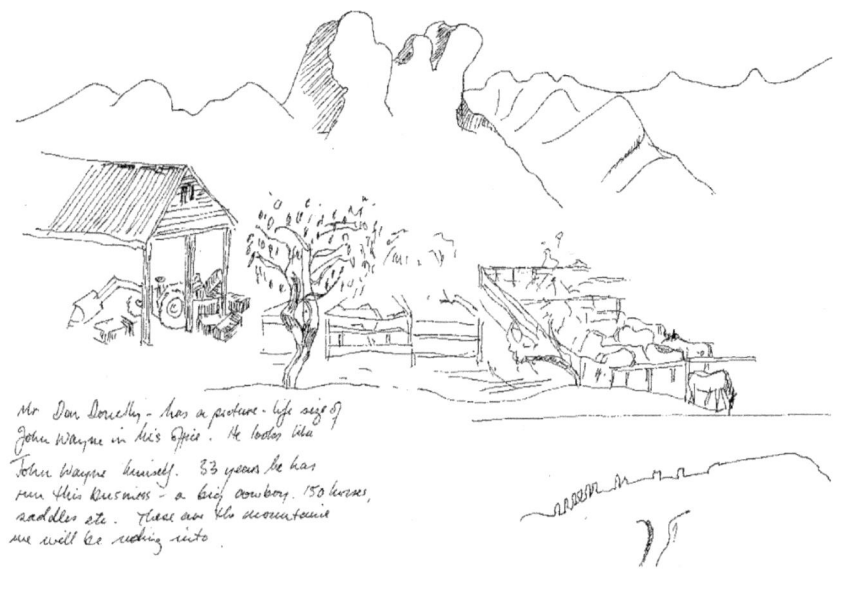

Mr Don Donelly - has a picture - life size of
John Wayne in his office. He looks like
John Wayne himself. 33 years he has
run this business - a brief cowboy. 150 horses,
saddles etc. These are the mountains
we will be riding into.

DON DONELLY'S RANCH

I have been covering the pond at night with a plank of wood to keep the raccoons out and deny them a fish supper. However their latest trick is to stretch their arms under the plank and try their luck at snatching the fish.

Last night their marauding arms grabbed my pots filled with water lillies. They pulled them up and threw them around the garden. They also grabbed the pump out of the pond and threw that away. They are determined to destroy everything within their grasp in their efforts to reach the fish.

Now it is war! John has been looking at ads for AK47's and giving me instructions on how I am to rent some more cages. Me, I don't think there's much point. I believe there's a continuous stream of racoons nearby moving down their own raccoon freeway from the inner city suburbs of Los Angeles where they once lived and can no longer. In any case I like them.

Every afternoon I feel so sick. The sickness carries on into the evening and is wearing me down. Along with feeling ill I keep thinking that I am a liability to all the healthy people in my life. I feel I'm only half in this world.

Sunday

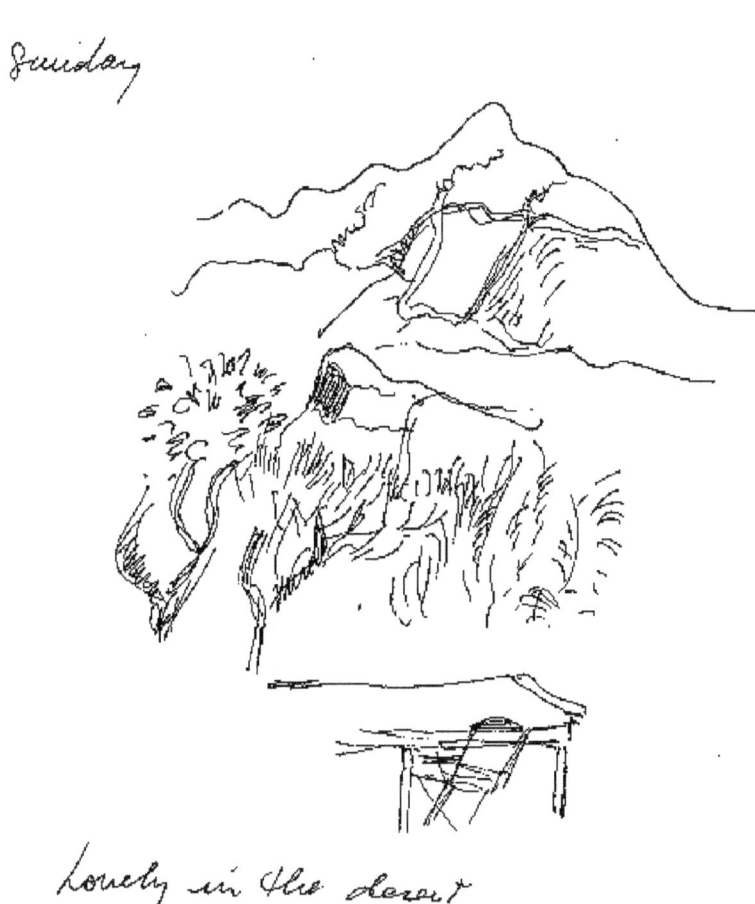

Lonely in the desert

SUPERSTITION MOUNTAINS

I don't want to identify with sick people. I refuse to join any survivor groups that everybody keeps suggesting to me. I want to belong to the healthy world not the unhealthy.

It's the Fourth of July in a few days and every night there are fireworks blasting around the house.

Two nights ago a firework landed on a house five blocks away and the house was burnt to the ground.

When I first came to America I was amazed at how much patriotism was displayed with the flying of flags from all the houses. I am less surprised now, although it still strikes me that the most prolific of the flag flyers are the houses inhabited with Mexican families. Annually on the Fourth they haul out their flags and proudly fly the stars and stripes.

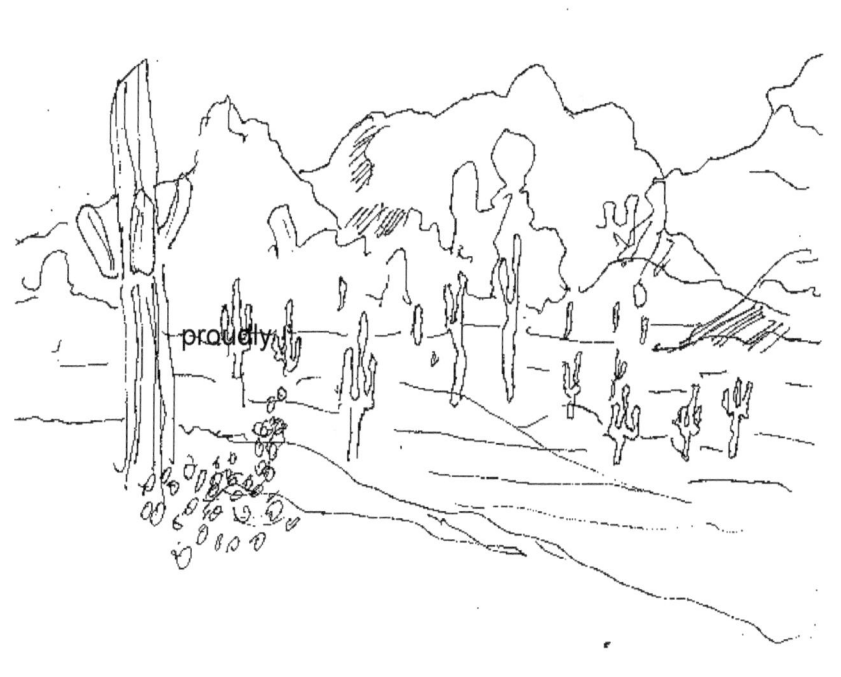

SUNSET

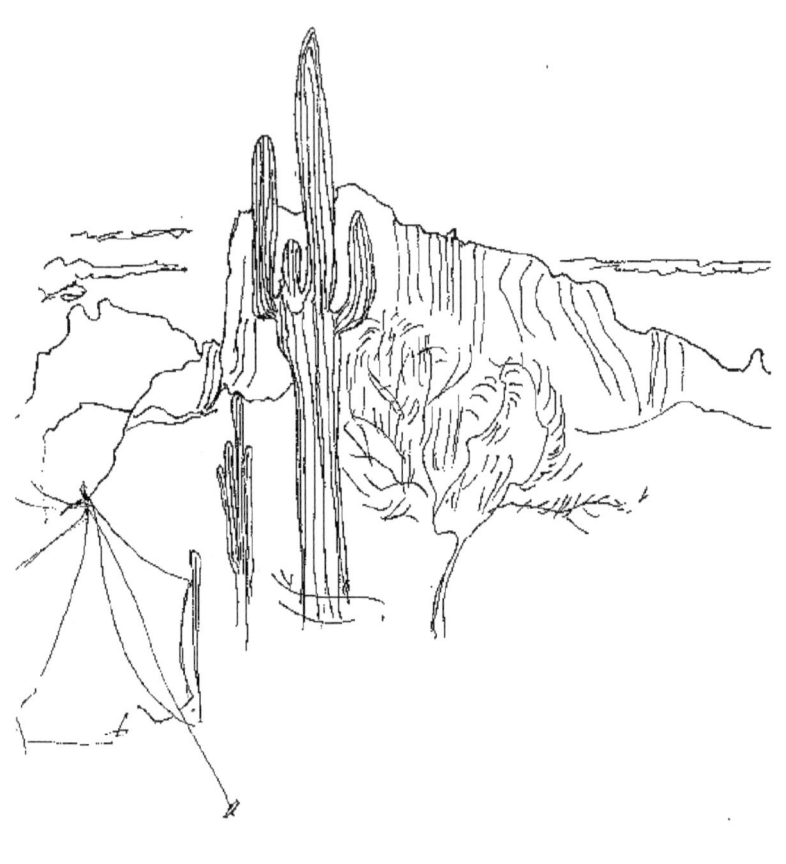

CAMP SUPERSTITION MOUNTAINS

Monday evening - back in camp after a challenging
and awe inspiring day. Started in the valley and climbed
up into Superstition Mountain - the horse climbed up &
down table sized boulders - sheer drops - narrow paths -
around, up & down - in eternity it seemed -
surrounded by mountains and rugged outcrops. The
only sounds were birds and the horses feet and breath
as they worked their way on treacherous paths.
Superstition mountains have claimed 65 lives this century
People love the trail and say they feel the mountains
have eyes that are watching them.
Now the colors hit the rock faces - showing every little
crevasse and scrub - the color is such a rich orange/red
with bright green cactus in front - The colors last a few
minutes only.

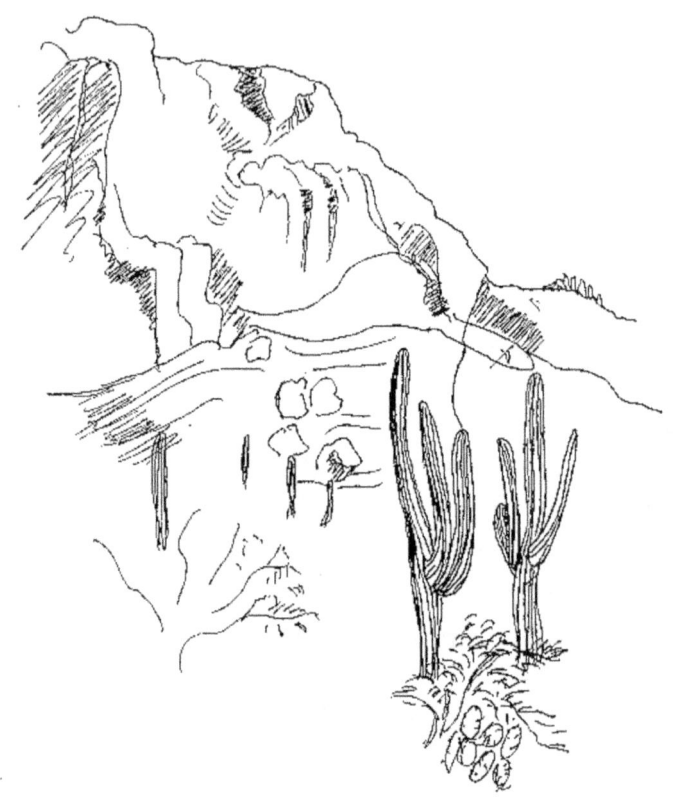

Monday morning – remember Cathy.
and courage. The breakfast gong rings!

MORNING

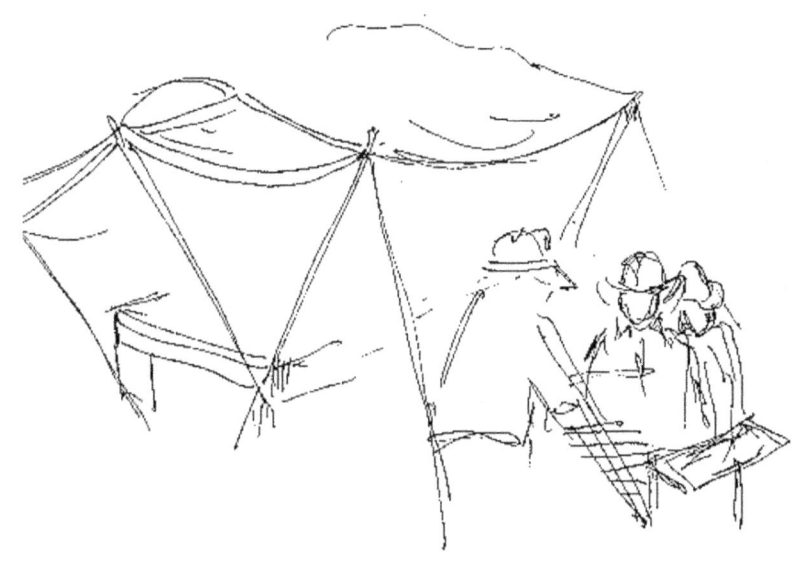

TIME TO EAT

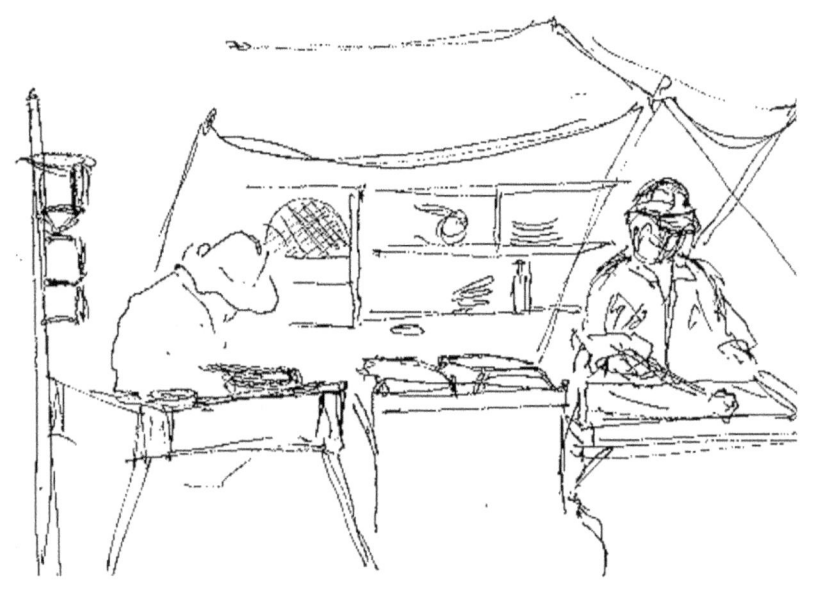

THE KITCHEN

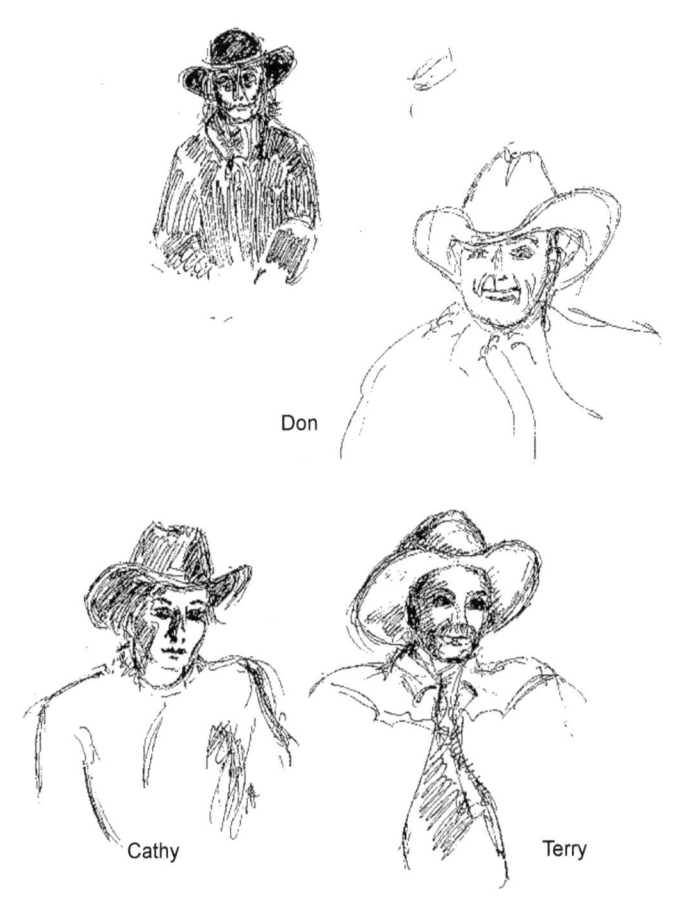

Don

Cathy

Terry

RIDE MATES

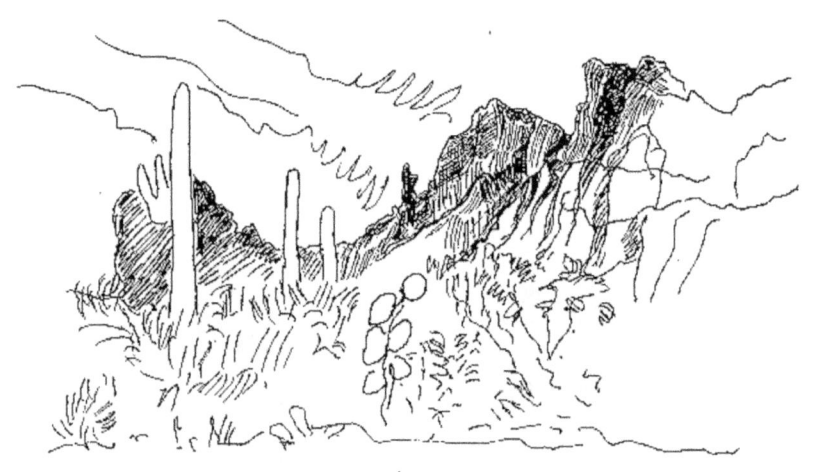

THE RIDE

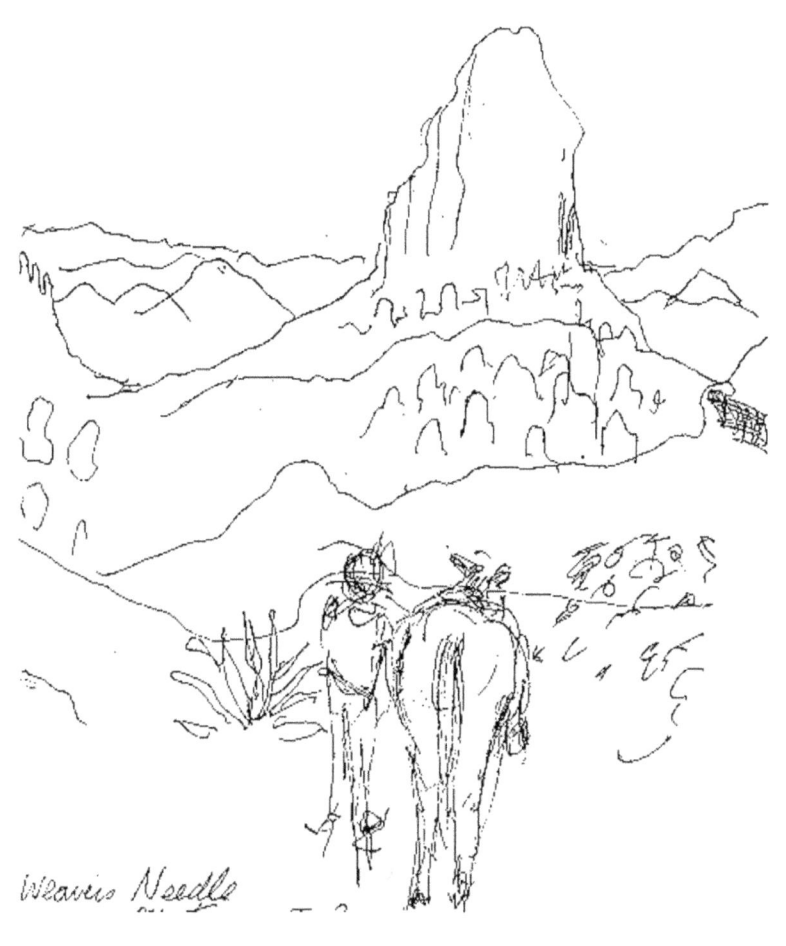

WEAVER'S NEEDLE

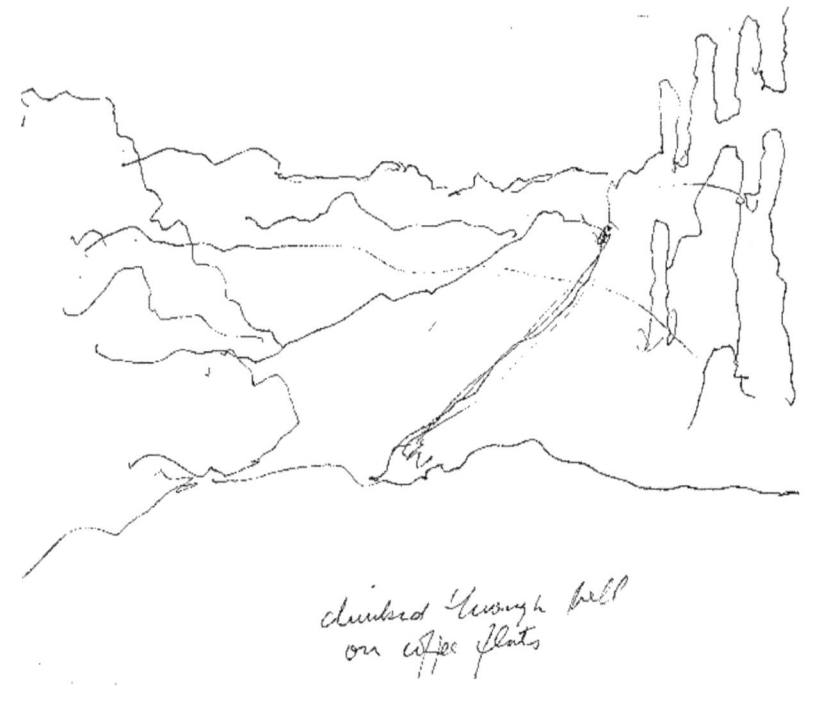

climbed through bell
on coffee flats

COFFEE FLATS

SUPERSTITION MOUNTAINS

"Terry, our leader, led us up Cofee Flats to Fremont Pass to Weavers Needle. Unbelievable terrain.

Narrow paths, giant steps over huge boulders, steep incline, horses puffing and panting, knuckles white."

Weaver was an army officer chasing Apaches. The rocks around are the Hohokam indians, turned to stone by the Gods 2000 years ago.

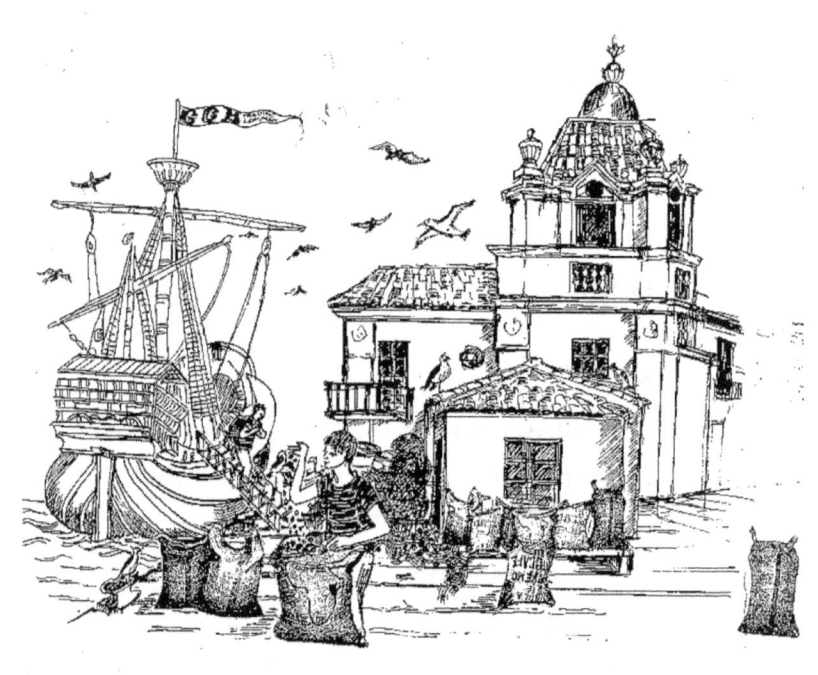

FISHERIES-SAN PEDRO

FOUND ON THE CLIFF AT
POINT FERMIN

As I reached the top of the cliff I looked around at the now misty Pacific Ocean. The sailboats that I had been looking at Near Catalina were now obscured by the grey cloud.

I started walking along the edge towards home and saw half hidden in the grass some slightly wilted white roses. A letter was wound around the stems. I carefully separated the letter from the roses and started reading the neat cursive writing.

"Dear Joseph,
I am feeling very lonely and wanted to tell you how much I miss you. I will be going away to college soon and I am scared of going. Everything seems to be so very hard and I wont know anybody there. I broke off with my boyfriend last week and that made me very sad. Everytime I look at the little fairy house that you gave me my eyes are full of tears and my heart hurts. I miss you so very much. It is a year now since you left this world and I miss you just as much now as then.
Love Mara.".

I refolded the letter and placed it carefully back with the white roses and looked over the cliff wondering why a 16 year old boy had the need to throw his life away.

Pain has always been a catalyst for me to write. It is a cathartic release for situations that have no clear resolutions.

www.ingramcontent.com/pod-product-compliance
Lightning Source LLC
Chambersburg PA
CBHW071642170526
45166CB00003B/1391